ENIO PECCHIONI

VIKINGS. THE ITALIAN SAGA

*Bjorn Ironside's journey
and the raid into the ancient Tuscany cities*

Press & Archeos

Press & Archeos
via Cittadella, 9
50144 Florence
www.pressandarcheos.com
info@pressandarcheos.com

Iconographic research by the author.
For other photos and illustrations, the publisher has taken care of the
relevant permissions from the rights holders. In the case of those whose
names were found to be unavailable, we remain available to settle any
claims.

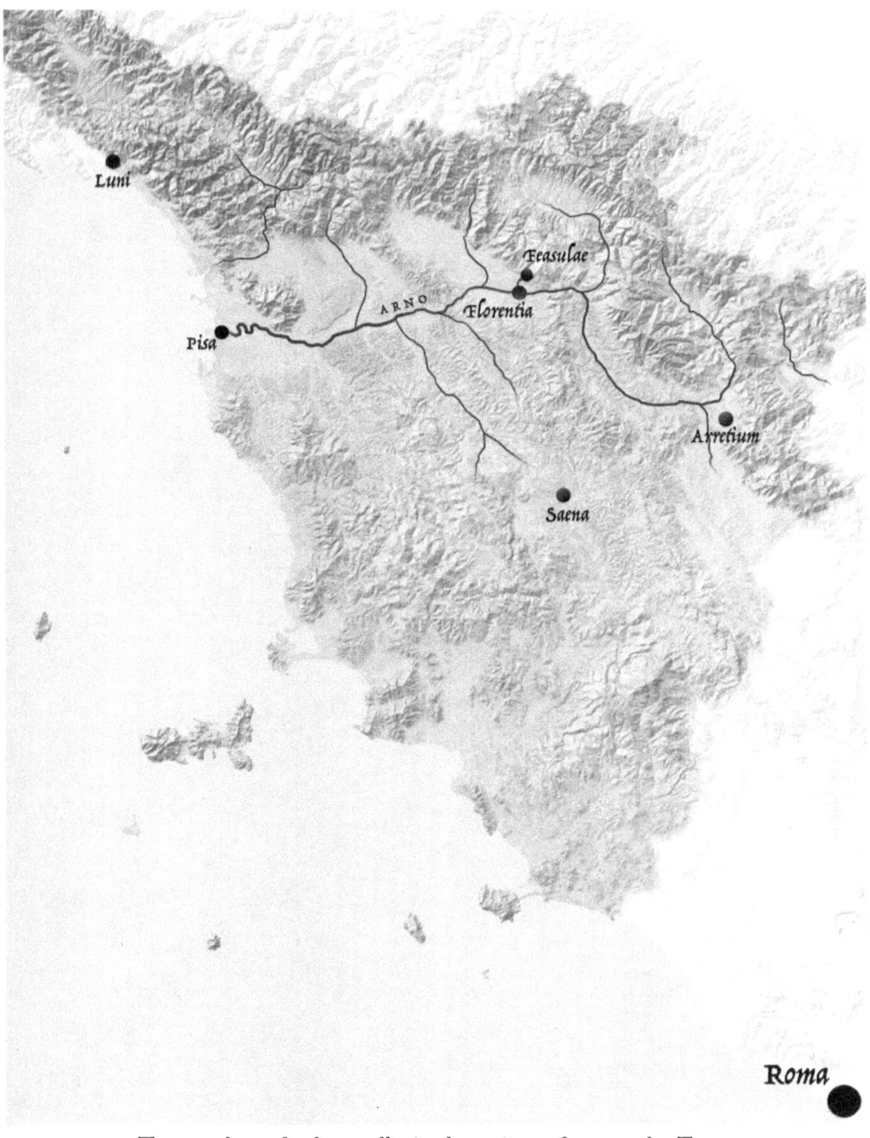

The map shows the Arno valley in the territory of present-day Tuscany, where the Viking raid took place in the year 860.

Rediscovering the Viking adventure in Tuscany

Thirty years have passed since the "Age of the Vikings" exhibition was held at the Ospedale degli Innocenti in Florence, showcasing a culture that was largely unknown to Italians.

The exhibition created awe and wonder, particularly with regard to the Vikings' naval adventures along the Arno River. However, little has been said or added since then.

In 860, a fleet of Viking ships entered the Mediterranean. After plundering the coasts of Spain and France, commanders Hastein and Bjørn Ironside decided to head for Tuscany.

After raiding Pisa, the Vikings sailed up the Arno River, reaching Florence and Fiesole. They conquered the city 'on the lunate hill', as well as the castle of Bishop Donatus at San Domenico.

The scarcity of medieval sources makes it difficult to gain insight into these events, but with a little imagination and using a method already employed in other publications, we will attempt to fill in the historical gaps and make these events more comprehensible.

We are talking about a fact that is as little known as it is surprising and significant: the daring expedition carried out by those rough northern sailors who were scornful of danger and would later participate in the cultural development of Europe.

The Author

" " Publius Cornelius Tacitus describes the Swedes as masters in the art of navigation:
«[Suiones] praeter viros armaque classibus valent. Forma navium eo differt, quod utrimque prora paratam semper appulsui frontem agit» [*De origine et situ Germanorum*, 44].
"This is the earliest literary affirmation of the Vikings' vocation for the sea, a trait that would develop over the following centuries ..."

VICHINGS

THE ITALIAN SAGA

The predators of the sea

The Vikings were descended from Germanic tribes that moved north into Scandinavia more than two thousand years ago. The name Vikings perhaps derives from an ancient Norwegian word which means "predators of the sea", and could be traced back to the verb *vige* (withdraw), indicating those who manage to escape with the loot of raids.

Skilled sailors and formidable warriors, the Vikings were also courageous and ruthless pirates who left their rocky fjords in search of fortune, heading everywhere. Their wanderings in the north of the Atlantic and their raids in Europe, known as the invasions of the Normans in France, Spain and Italy, and of the Varangians or Rus in Russia, left an indelible mark on the collective imagination, inspiring many fantastic stories. The Northmen were the Scandinavian populations who migrated to northern Europe in the High Middle Ages, while the name 'Normanni' came to refer specifically to the Norwegian raiders who settled in Normandy in the eighth century.

Germans of lineage, robust and enterprising, greedy for wealth and power ... among the Vikings the rule of force was legally recognised, and the weak did not have the right to own goods since they could not defend them. The bravest warrior gained social support, and only the king had decision-making authority in political or religious matters.

Within the Norman family, the father's authority was unquestioned, unless he suddenly lost his status. Polygamy was not uncommon among the Vikings, and, as reported by tenth-century Arab writer Ibn Fadlan, they were not ashamed to have sexual relations with a slave on duty in front of their companions. Laws and sentences were promulgated with the affirmation of a popular assembly called the Thing, which met in each Viking region. The meetings took place at regular intervals and at certain times the assembly could elect a king. Women too could assume leadership roles, become aristocrats or even queens. They could therefore obtain a divorce from their spouse with the attached material goods owned by them.

Furthermore, the Vikings (like the Etruscans and other European peoples already) burned their dead. The Arab writer Ibn Fadlan, who attended a Viking funeral ceremony, was told: «... *you Arabs are barbarians, you take the people you love and put them underground to feed worms, we, on the other hand, burn those we love so that they can enter Paradise at once*».[1]

The necessity of raids

The poverty of the original locations, the excessive number of inhabitants (also due to widespread polygamy), and the meager fruits of agriculture and pastoralism, drove the Vikings to navigation for the purpose of prey and trade. Increasingly skilled navigators, they sailed the seas of northern Europe and the Atlantic on agile vessels.

In the 9th century, internecine wars, which led to the establishment of large kingdoms in Sweden, Norway and Denmark, prompted many to seek new lands in which to settle. The Normans thus penetrated the various countries by sailing their shallow draft ships up the course of rivers, and brought terror to the European hinterland.

The Norman hulls, with their dragon-shaped figureheads, would suddenly spring up in the river ports of the cities, and before an organized defense was possible, the warriors were ashore ready to attack those who stood before them; they abused the young women whom they then dragged along with them, stowed away the ships of booty, and resumed the sea. A few hours after the assault they had already disappeared.

As time passed, the invasions no longer presented these negative effects. Continued incursions caused certain areas of the con-

---

[1] Ibn Fadlan, *Embassy diary*, X sec., cfr. BRØNDSTED 2001, p. 303.

A Viking commander scans the sea from his snekke in a 20th-century illustration. Although they are traditionally depicted wearing horned helmets, Vikings probably wore no such head-gear, because nothing similar appears in the iconographies of the time.

tinent to become zones of occupation and settlement where they exercised military and political dominance with inevitable diplomatic relations with other peoples and mutual cultural influences.

In the occupied places the Vikings built small towns or trading bases; these towns, which rarely exceeded two thousand inhabitants, generally stood on the seashore or at least along a waterway so that ships could moor to load and unload goods. The settlements were protected by fortifications consisting of an embankment and a palisade. Typical were the farms, built in the inland territories in one large building, a "long house" that could be up to thirty meters long, built of ash wood with a loggia around it, in which masters and servants lived together.

*Odin with his sacred ravens and the wolves Geri and Freki. There is
no lack of the dragon icon that appeared in all Norse ships.*

Norman cosmology

The Vikings interpreted the universe as composed of several
separate worlds and supported by a giant ash tree (Yggdrasil), or
a yew or an oak tree, however sacred trees among the peoples of
northern Europe. The world of the gods was called Asgard, here
was the great hall known as Valhalla, the place where warriors
who died in battle were rewarded with banquets of honor.

Like the Greek, Etruscan and Roman religions, the Nordic
religion was polytheistic. Numerous gods were venerated, each
of which presided over a particular human activity or need. The
main divinity was Wotan (Odin), father of all gods, a splendid,
imposing, demonic and cruel figure, always accompanied by two
faithful crows on his shoulders: Hugin, which means "thought"

and Mugin which means "memory". Every day the crows flew over the world and in the evening they returned to the god to tell him what they had seen.

Odin had Frigg as his wife, and a son, Balder: Frigg also appears as a mother and is said to have had the power of clairvoyance. Balder was the deity of benevolence: his figure and myth suggest a connection with the Sun.

Thor was the god of thunder. At the command of his parade of goats he "rolled" through the clouds making a racket from hell; like most of his human followers he loved to laugh and have fun, but he was of a touchy nature and easy to anger. The twins Frey and Freya were the god and goddess of fertility and love. Then there was Loki, wicked instigator of dissension. Around these dominant figures gravitated a host of lesser gods, elves, and genies who often embodied the souls of the dead.

As for language, it must be said that the Vikings used, in their short inscriptions, the runic script assimilated by the Celtic peoples and derived from Etruscan. The basic alphabet, called futhark from its first six letters but originally of twenty-four, became in the ninth century of sixteen letters.

It is thought that the Vikings attributed magical powers to the words such that warriors very often inlaid runes on the blades of their swords.

The ship, temple of the Vikings

Without going into details, given the important publications devoted to the subject,[2] we report some facts about the ships of the Vikings and their methods of navigation.

The ship is the pinnacle of technical skill and knowledge of the peoples of northern Europe. For the Vikings, these were in-

---

[2] Among the many we mention Eldar Heide, *The early Viking Ship Types* (2014) or the fabulous two-part novel by Frans Bengtsson, *The Long Ships* (1945).

Gokstad's ship, discovered in 1880 near a Norwegian farm in Vestfold og Telemark county.

struments of power, their most cherished possession...what for the Greeks were temples, for the Vikings were ships. The heart of the Vikings belonged to the sea. They were the most skilled and daring sea racers of their time, and their ships were among the most beautiful and felicitous creations of all nautical construction art.

Viking fleets were a rather heterogeneous collection of vessels aimed at specific uses but united by a uniform line: slender and flexible, keel-rigged and with symmetrical ends. The construction type was based on overlapping planking with planks riveted together. It is inferred from literary sources and archaeological findings that all or most boats had bow and stern figureheads in the shape of a dragon's head (drakkar) or griffin.[3] These decorations had an apotropaic function, to frighten the enemy but also to keep at bay the sea monsters that, according to Norse mythology, populated the sea.

Ships were used for a variety of purposes: wartime raids (landings and amphibious operations), short- and long-distance trade, exploration, and colonization. In the literature, Viking ships are generally divided into two broad categories: merchant ships (knarr) and warships (drakkar), which are actually overlapping. In fact, some types of merchant ships, built specifically to transport goods, could be reconfigured into warships.

---

[3] From the griffin, a large carnivorous predatory bird, they would come to draw the Viking griffin, which was used especially in small decorations; but there are those who claim it is a stylization of the lion figure, borrowed from Frankish miniaturists.

The spectacle of Viking ships landing, on the verge of a great raid, in a 20th-century illustration.

Most Viking ships were designed to navigate rivers, fjords, and coastal waters (snekke), while others (knarr)[4] could navigate the open sea and even the ocean. They could reverse course without having to turn around; the symmetry between the bow and stern allowed them to change course simply by paddling in the opposite direction.

It is thought that the wheel keel of Viking vessels was preserved generation after generation and that the ship was rebuilt on it; this was not only as a traditional-religious matter, but also because reusing a keel in good condition brought savings in time and money. In general, a typical 23-meter ship required at least eleven masts of about ninety centimeters in diameter for its construction, plus another mast that served as a rudder, secured with leather stays on the starboard side. The rudder was thus a single piece of oak wood, made like the blade of a huge oar, such that it

---

[4] The knarr had a shorter and wider hull, thus with more draft.

could be steered in all kinds of weather conditions.

The ships had a single mast that could be reclined, with a wind vane at the top. The mast supported a large square or rectangular sail woven in double thickness of coarse wool or linen, often colored in red and blue stripes. Sagas and other literary sources also record completely red ones. In headwinds, flat calm, or to give the assault, the Vikings used oars. Sitting on crates that contained their belongings, sailors would stick their oars into rowing holes drilled in the sides and then row hard and in cadence.

To chart courses on the high seas, navigators relied almost exclusively on the sun, moon and stars: particularly uncertain indicators that often disappeared behind a dark veil of fog. But in all Viking vessels there was always on board a primordial astrolabe, consisting of a wooden disk floating in a container of water with a vertical rod that calculated, based on the length of the shadow, the height of the sun. They also had on board the so-called "sun stone", the cordierite, a kind of crystal that possesses the property of changing color from yellow to blue when exposed perpendicular to the plane of sunlight. By polarizing the refraction of light it made it possible to locate the position of the star on cloudy or foggy days, thus enabling orientation.

Safe orientation points existed only in coastal navigation, and they were either natural or man-made: mountains, bays or islands, lone trees, crosses or stone milestones. Experienced sailors were able to determine the ship's course based on wind direction, sea currents and simple wave motion. But if they ran into bad weather, a storm, even they had to rely more on luck than instinct. There was always a large waxed tent on board that sailors could spread out to cover the deck, to shelter from rain or sun. Ships carried a sturdy iron anchor and a small four-oared lifeboat (faering) that was used for fishing, as a rescue, or as a shuttle.

According to legends, Viking navigators used to carry caged ravens on board, used in case they got lost. These animals would be able to find land again by guiding the boat and its crew to safe-

The Return of the Vikings, painting by John Harris Valda (1874-1942).

ty. The sighting of a whale also made it possible to determine the right direction since whales for feeding are wont to be stationed in waters not far from land.

There were no hearths aboard Viking ships. If cooking was required, it was done at landfall, on land. Large pots were placed on the fire that hung from a modular iron tripod. Oatmeal or at best boiled meat was consumed, while on board one was content with cold foods: galettes, stockfish, herrings, smoked bacon, nuts, apples, aged cheese, dried meat, mead, which was stored in leather flasks, and beer contained in kegs.

As we can see, it was a fairly lean diet, which explains how so many pirate actions were necessary first and foremost for the search for food, mainly fresh meat. It seems that boiled meat was preferred to roast; in fact, boiled meat from the Saehrimni pig was offered to the chosen warriors in Valhalla.

The extraordinarily pliable ships allowed the Vikings to winter in the heart of enemy territory. Once anchored in the middle of a river they were unassailable, as well as on river islands, where they liked to place their winter quarters....

Vikings effortlessly would glide with their "nut shells" over the shallow sandy bottoms, leaving the enemy in the lurch. As handed down by the monk chronicler Nestor of Kiev, the Vikings were able to overcome the barrages of rivers and sea stretches by grounding their ships and sliding them over polished logs or dragging them on wheels, as happened with the barrier on the Bosporus built by the Byzantines during the siege of Constantinople in 907.

An essential feature of Viking seamanship was undoubtedly speed. The Vikings were able to sail from Scandinavia to North America in less than a month. The navigator Gunnbiørn came within sight of Greenland around 920; the Canadian coast was discovered by chance in 985 by a lost sailor whose name was Bjar-

Above, a so-called "Wall of Shields" during a reenactment dedicated to the Vikings (photo by Hans S, CC 2.0). Below, reconstruction of a Viking shield (photo by Peer.Gynt, CC 2.0).

ni Herjolfsson.[5]

The discovery of 11th-century Viking graves at L'Anse aux Meadows in northern Newfoundland in 1961 provided proof of the accuracy of the Viking sagas concerning the land of Vinland. It is now certain that the Vikings came not only to Greenland, but also to Canada and thus to America.

---

[5] As he proceeded to Greenland to join his father Herjolf, Bjarni Herjolfsson's ships were blown off course by the storm until they skirted the new lands of the American continent: "mountainous, forest-covered land with low hills" (Gwyn 1977, p. 316).

A Viking burial ceremony with related "funeral ship," in a painting by Heinrich Semiradzki (1845–1902).

Björn "Ironside" and the leader Hastein

Björn and his brothers

Firstly, it is important to note that both Bjørn and Hastein are notable figures and among the most prominent and ambitious Viking leaders of the 9th century. Their exploits in the Mare di Mezzo (the Mediterranean), recounted by various historians, are largely fantastic. It is a story that fits into the legend of the greatest of the Vikings, Ragnar Lodbrok, king of Sweden and Denmark. History and fiction blend together in medieval literature, inspiring contemporary publishing and cinema.

One version of the Saga of the Sons of Ragnar relates that Bjørn Jaernsida ("Iron side or Iron hips") was the son of the Swedish king Ragnar Lodbrok ("Hairy breeches") and together with some brothers set out from Sweden to conquer the Jutland peninsula in Denmark, settling in Leire under the orders of his brother Ivar ("Boneless").[6]

Ragnar Lodbrok, envious of these conquests, placed Eysteinn Beli as his vassal on the throne of Sweden to defend it from his sons, so he crossed the Baltic to the east to raid. Shortly afterwards Eiríkr and Agnar, two half-brothers of Bjørn, landed in Sweden and sent Eysteinn a request for submission, asking Eysteinn's daughter Borghild to marry for Eiríkr. Eysteinn, having consulted the clan leaders, refused the proposal. A clash followed that saw Eiríkr and Agnar overwhelmed by Swedish forces: the former fell prisoner and the latter died.

Bjørn and another brother, upset by the news, set sail for Sweden with a large army, and during a great battle Eysteinn

---

[6] An important saga dedicated to Ragnar Lodbrok is related by Saxo Grammaticus, a 12th-century Danish historian and theologian, in his Gesta Danorum.

*A Viking captain leads the landing on a frozen land, in an illu-
stration with dubious iconography (20th century).*

was killed.

Ragnar Lodbrok was not happy that his sons had taken justice
into their own hands, but it seems that his interests were already
directed elsewhere. In command of only two knarr he decided to
resume his raids into England. Defeated by Ella of Northumbria
he was thrown into a pit of poisonous snakes where, seizing on
the irony of fate, he died singing and in great laughter.

Bjørn and the brothers swore revenge on the Saxons of Northumbria. As soon as possible they attacked King Ella but were
repulsed. In the following months Ivar asked Ella for peace and a
ransom for the killing of his father and succeeded in obtaining an

arm of land where he founded the city of York. In this way Ivar made himself popular in England. At a later time he called on his brothers to prepare a new attack. In the battle he was thus able to take their side, together with many English chieftains, with their respective people loyal to the Vikings in tow. Ella was captured and killed with a heavy torment: his chest was opened with a hot iron and his lungs torn out, according to a bloody Viking ritual.[7]

Hastein the "mentor"

Little is known of the early life of Hastein, described as a Dane in various chronicles and often considered himself the son of Ragnar Lodbrok. He is mentioned, on a first occasion, as taking part in a Viking attack on the Frankish Kingdom by occupying the island of Noirmoutier, in 843.[8] He appears again in the Loire in 859, at the beginning of the great raid that continued in the Mediterranean together with Bjørn the Ironsides.

According to the Gesta Normannorum of William of Jumièges (11th century) Denmark had too much population due to the habit of men to take several wives, for which a law was imposed according to which all children were to be expelled, except the one who was recognized as heir.

Among the young expellees was also Bjørn Fianchi di Ferro who left the country with his pedagogus[9] Hastein. Inspired by his father Ragnar's mythical raid years earlier in Paris, Bjørn

---

[7] Ragnar's sons "engraved" the blood eagle on Ella's back: the rite consisted in separating the victim's ribs from the spine and then extracting the lungs by spreading them across the back, styling them like wings (Gwyn 1977, p. 231 , note 12).

[8] Hastein probably also occupied the island of Groix on the coast of Brittany, slightly south of the mouth of the Loire, to ensure control of the salt route so important in the economy of the peoples.

[9] This is how William of Jumièges, a Norman monk and historian of the 11th century, defines it. An odd term in this context, as it would mean a guide or teacher to a schoolboy; but perhaps Hastein was meant to be understood as a kind of mentor, a wise and trusted adviser with paternal authority.

launched a new attack against the city on the Seine. He therefore occupied the abbey of St. Denis and the Franks, to dislodge the invaders, were forced to pay an incredible sum in gold and silver.

After the enterprise in the Mediterranean Hastein made his appearance in Brittany. In 866 he allied himself with King Solomon against the Franks and, with the Viking-Breton army, defeated Robert the Strong at the battle of Brissarthe. In 872, after a moment of truce, he went up the Loire occupying Angers, where he was besieged by the Frankish king Charles the Bald who with a series of barriers along the rivers prevented him from any possibility of escape. Hastein was then forced to make a peace, in October 873.

Hastein remained in French territory for many more years, raging between the Loire and the Seine, until he set his sights on the riches of England and set sail with a new army. In England his ruthlessness and his experience in military tactics led to successes, but also defeats. The Viking army dispersed into East Anglia and Northumbria in the spring of 896.

At this point Hastein disappeared from history, deservedly remaining in Viking chronicles as one of the most famous warlords in history.

Shipping to the Mediterranean

The historical context

The ancient Roman Empire was long gone, but many in the Middle Ages saw Charlemagne as the man who could restore imperial authority and ensure the peaceful coexistence and progress of Christian peoples.

Following his great military victories and expansion of his territory, Charlemagne divided the Carolingian Empire into counties at the end of the 8th century. Each county included a city and its district. In border territories, where defence was necessary, several counties were grouped together to form a 'Marca'.

Counts and marquises were put in charge of the counties and marches and governed in the name of the emperor. The Church was closely united with the state and placed under the protection of the sovereign; other powers, of various kinds, were also entrusted to bishops and abbots who often considered themselves imperial officials, in some cases with the title of count.

The Carolingian Empire was short-lived. A few decades after the death of Charlemagne (814), that aggregate of different peoples that the emperor's high prestige had held together dissolved, opening a period of uncertainty, of dynastic disputes between heirs, descendants and various pretenders. In summary, after the deposition of the last Carolingian, the helpless Charles the Fat (887), France, Italy and Germany began to have their own history and to have their own rulers. It was in that period that goes roughly from the 9th to the 11th century, in the height of the so-called feudalism, that new people were seen roaming Europe: the Vikings.

According to a legend already Charlemagne, while he was in an unspecified point in the south of France, saw with great amazement appear in front of the coast, and disappear within a short time, a large fleet of ships with the dragon.

A similar vision of Nordic ships with the dragon also impressed an Arab chronicler who witnessed the passage of a Viking squadron with large rectangular sails, so much so that he suggested the comparison with "a flock of amaranth-colored seabirds".

In 827 the "seabirds" had already raided the kingdom of Asturias (northern Spain). A second expedition is recorded in 844, when a Viking fleet of fifty-four ships attacked, on the Bay of Biscay, Gijon in Asturias and soon after La Coruña in Galicia. But the inhabitants forcing the Vikings to retire in their boats and set sail again. Descending along the coast, they besieged Lisbon for thirteen days, attacked the city of Cadiz, seriously damaging it, and penetrated the interior by land up to the military bulwark of Medina Sidonia.

Having reached the mouth of the Guadalquivir, they went up the river to the Emirate of Cordoba, until they occupied Seville for a few weeks, setting fire to the great mosque, until the emir Abd al Rhaman II, having gathered his forces, managed to drive them out by burning many ships. The Arab writers Ibn al-Khutia and Ibn Adhari report that the emir sent 200 severed heads to Tangier as a pledge of his victory. At this point the luck of the Vikings changed: after the defeat they were happy to return part of the prisoners in exchange for supplies and fine clothes, and in short the entire fleet headed for the country of origin on the northern French coasts.[10]

As we have seen, the Vikings were therefore not afraid to attack territories already firmly conquered by the Muslims, who

---

[10] The Vikings called the Saracens "black men" and sold them as slaves even in faraway Ireland. But in Andalusia they took a beating from the "Moors", who managed by ambush to annihilate a large group of madjus (barbaric sorcerers, as the Arabs called the Vikings). Capturing some prisoners, they hanged or slit their throats without any fear of reprisals. Later history will show more conciliatory situations between the two ethnic groups, as was the case during the reign of the Norman William II of Altavilla, king of Sicily known as the Good (1153-1189): "The king of Sicily is unique for his good behavior and because he uses Muslims a lot and has Muslim eunuchs as pages. Many of them hide their faith, but respect the law of Islam. The king trusts Muslims a lot and he relies on them in his affairs and in the most important things to such an extent that the superintendent of his Curia is a Muslim..." (testimony of the Andalusian traveler Ibn Giubair, taken from Delogu 1990, p. 209).

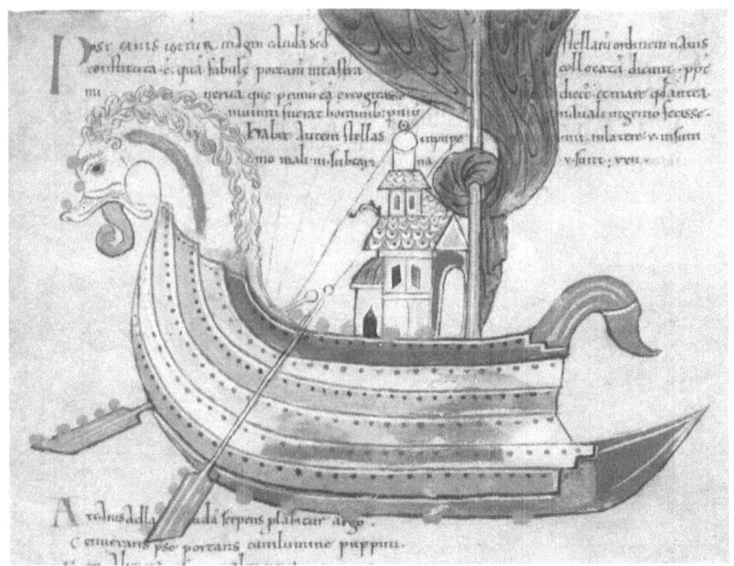

A Viking ship with dragon from a 14th century illuminated codex.

were equally ferocious and determined in their warlike actions and whose contempt for death was equally unlimited.

Fifteen years after the last incursion, what was probably an old dream of the Vikings, came true: to penetrate the Mediterranean Sea in the direction of Rome.

The context in which the Viking raids in Italy took place was that of the great expedition which took place between 859 and 861, led by Count Hastein and Bjørn Jaernsida ("Iron Sides"), an undertaking that lasted three years and was considered one of the most daring of this people. Hastein and Bjørn, to carry out the feat, left other captains during yet another raid in French territory, on the Seine up to Paris. From their fortified hideout on the Isle of Thanet (in southeast England, now a peninsula) they set sail with 62 ships and just over a thousand intrepid warriors. After carrying out some quick looting in the Aquitaine Basin, where

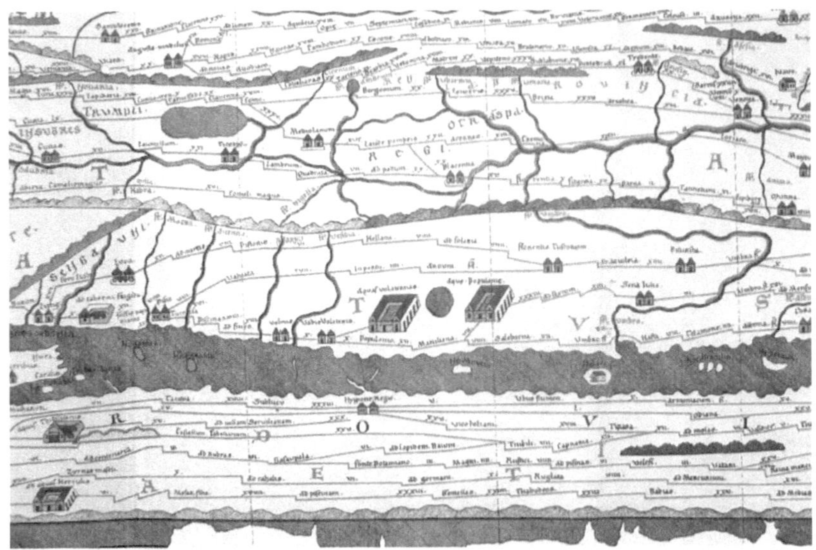

In the Peutingeriana Table, a 12th-13th century copy of a Roman-era map; the cities of Tuscia affected by Viking and Saracen raids are clearly recognized.

they operated going up the Garonne, the Vikings skirted the Cantabrian and Iberian area reaching the Strait of Gibraltar. Here they ravaged Algeciras and its mosque, and entered the Mediterranean Sea.

According to Arab historians Al Bakri and Ibn Idhari, Hastein's corsairs, who dreamed of giving the younger Bjørn the dignity of Roman emperor, plundered the kingdom of Nekor in the Moroccan Rif; they plundered the Balearic Islands (at that time they were already in the hands of Saracen pirates) and devastated Roussillon, on the border between the Iberian Peninsula and France.

After wintering in the Rhone delta, settling on Camargue Island, in the spring of 860 they began their ascent up the river. They set fire to Arelate (Arles) and sacked Nimes, before finally destroying Valence, in the Dauphiné, a two hundred kilometers from the mouth. But here they suffered considerable losses caused by the army of Gerard of Provence or of Roussillon, Count of Vienne, whose deeds are sung by the Benedictine monk Abbone of San Germano, in his De bellis Parisiacae urbis (at the turn of the 9th/10th century).

At this point, always numerous and enraged, they went back down the Rhone, abandoned the camp at the mouth and pointed their ships towards the coasts of Tuscia: «allured by the flattering prospect of rapid and substantial booty».

Leaving Provence the ships of the Vikings resumed traveling the sea.

The intentions of Bjørn and Hastein had been clarified in the previous evenings during some meetings in the camp in the Camargue, where the invaders stopped to regroup after the defeat in the Dauphiné. The raids had produced a good amount of supplies and it really seemed possible to look out over the coasts of that peninsula called Italy, pointing to places of great fame, perhaps Rome itself, of which the Viking captains had a fantastic, distorted as well as fascinating vision.

Suggested by the few maps available and having ascertained the coastline, the navigators of the north, apparently accustomed to very different distances and dangers, thought of shortening the journey by going from the open sea, to buy time and be able to play by surprise. They didn't know how even that stretch of sea can be difficult at certain times of the year.

In the middle of the Ligurian sea a tense and changeable wind began to rise which did not bode well. Oars had to be used to steer the course. In the early hours of the evening the wind suddenly strengthened, pulling low and dark clouds behind it: a storm was fast approaching. Soon the waters stirred. The wind carried masses of water beyond the bow figurehead and the waves grew more and more. Amidst the roar of the waves could be heard the cries of Hastein and young Bjørn, each on his own ship, directed at their sailors who had worked hard to lower the knarr's sails.

The ships skittered like fish, appearing and disappearing in the momentary moonlight among gigantic waves. It would have been difficult to guess that a stretch of sea like this, relatively short, could be so dangerous! The ships lost sight of each other and some companions fell into the water, with no possibility of rescue. But the phenomenon was as intense as it was brief. Entering the heart of the Tyrrhenian sea, the waters were already stretched out, while the lights of dawn began to manifest themselves. The ships mustered: none had been lost. The Viking woods continued their descent longitudinally, towards the coasts of Tuscia.

Bjørn observed the first image of that longed-for land, known only through stories and some ancient maps. Who knows if the men of Italy had any awareness of the danger they were about to run, if the Christian God was ready to meet the fury of Odin... If ever there had been heard of the Vikings.

But that mission didn't just have a raiding function: it was an important exploration initiative, a face-to-face challenge with the gods.

In Europe, the coming of the Vikings and their bloody deeds were read, in that historical moment, with anguished accents, as if they heralded the end of the world. The chronicles are full of apocalyptic and infernal images: fires in the form of dragons, terrible hurricanes, hordes of ravenous wolves, huge comets harbinger of doom.

The Vikings are interpreted, also in a prophetic sense, as instruments of divine wrath, aimed at the punishment of the sins of Christians: "*The Viking predatory pagans instruments of God's wrath will come with enormous numbers of ships to kill the people of Christ and to destroy lands and goods with sword and fire*". So declaimed Alcuin, adviser to Charlemagne, echoed by Prudentius of Troyes in the Annales Bertiniani.

The Viking raids extended to places incredibly distant from the homeland, where it is suggestive to imagine the landing of men of the North, as described in this nineteenth-century illustration.

The Legend of the Sack of Luni

From the 8th to the 10th century, there were frequent pirate attacks along the Tyrrhenian coast.

In 727, the Saracens devastated the monastery of San Mamiliano on Montecristo Island. During this period, monastic life also disappeared from Capraia and Gorgona, probably due to similar attacks.

Tarquinia, an ancient Etruscan city, was abandoned in the 8th century following numerous raids. The population then moved to the hill adjoining the ancient city and erected the fortress of Corneto, on which the present city stands. Populonia suffered the same fate in 809, with the subsequent abandonment of the city in the following decades and the transfer of the episcopal see to Massa Marittima in 842. It was also decided in that year to move the relics of St. Cerbone, the patron saint and bishop of Populonia.

In 846 the Saracens attacked Rome.

In 849, or for others in 860, it was Luni's turn, important city located on the current border between Tuscany and Liguria. Some authors attribute this assault to the Vikings.

Pirate assaults along the Tyrrhenian coast started from Sicily and were the exclusive prerogative of the Saracens. The action of the Vikings in Tuscany was a unique and sporadic case, however significant of their ardor, if one considers that after entering the Mediterranean they had already had the courage to assault Majorca, a possession of the most aggressive Muslims.

It was Dean Dudon of St. Quentin, in his Historia Normannorum (11th cent.), who devoted a circumstantial report to the taking of Luni, highlighting the unscrupulousness in the Viking's conduct of warfare. According to legend the raid took place in total geographical misunderstanding: basically, the Vikings allegedly misunderstood their maps and the few indications they had, thinking they were elsewhere.

Having landed on the Tuscan coast (or, according to some, af-

Representation of the Battle of Swolder, which took place in the western Baltic Sea in September 999.

ter sacking inland cities and then descending the Arno to the sea) the Viking pirates arrived before the territory of Luni. It is said that the town was so resplendent with light reflected from the numerous marble buildings that the invaders believed they were facing Rome.

The captains of Luni, frightened by the unexpected and threatening attack, deployed their troops along the coast and also hastily armed many citizens.

All that remains today are ruins of what was once a powerful maritime city. A thriving Etruscan center controlled by native peoples (Ligurians), with the Roman conquest it became first a military port, then a colony. In late Roman times the silting up of the port and the swamping of the coastal strip began with the slow decay of the city. Sacked by the Goths, it was reoccupied in 522 by the Eastern Romans/Byzantines.

It was Longobard rule, but it was under the Carolingian emperors that the city recovered to still be a commercial center with important bishopric, with many monuments and surrounded by solid walls.

The Viking leader Hastein, realizing the impossibility of taking the city by force of arms, resorted to a ruse: he sent a messenger to the burgrave and bishop of the city. Thus was declared, in the presence of the dignitaries, the peaceful intention of the Vikings.

"Hastein and his Danes, and all those whom fate has driven out of Denmark, greet you.

To you it is not unknown how, wandering through the stormy sea, we landed at the kingdom of the Franks. Into which penetrated we have, after many battles against the Frankish peoples, subdued their land to our chief. And desiring us, when we had completed the conquest, to return to the ancestral country, first blew the north wind against us, then prostrated those adverse from the west and south; Driven by the storm and not of our own will, we reached your coast.

We pray you now to grant us peace, that we may acquire provisions. Our duke is ill. Prostrate with grief, he wishes to receive baptism from you; moreover, should he in his extreme weakness be taken from us prematurely, he implores from your charity and mercy a worthy burial within your walls."

Before long the bishop and the count of the city replied, through their herald, making themselves available for the baptism of the duke and to allow the purchase of provisions.

Bishop Petroaldus prepared the baptismal font in the Plebs Civitatis, consecrated the water and had the candles lit.

Hastein arrived accompanied by Bjørn and a few Viking leaders. He was made to undress and helped down into the large pool. The bishop, proud that he could redeem a Viking chieftain, began the ceremony with great pomp. Immediately after receiving the baptism, the Norse were led back to their ship, with the captain gasping from illness.

As soon as he arrived at the ship Hastein gathered his subordinates and explained the second phase of his cunning, a shameful design of his own invention:

"Next you will announce my death to the bishop and pray amid tears that I be allowed to be buried in the city. In return promise him my swords, my buckles and everything that belongs to me."

Having said this, the Vikings hurried weeping before the lords of the city and then returned to report the success of the fraud.

Hastein reconvened the leaders of the various tribes and said to them:

"Make me a coffin quickly, place me as a corpse but with weapons beside me, and line up all around as in mourning but with axes well concealed. The others will launch the war cry in the streets, in the camp and on the ships."

At the order, sitting down, preparations began. The drums began to clatter. The wailing of the Vikings resounded all around, while the city bells called the people to the cathedral.

Having received the coffin on the beach from the Christians, with the pagans in tow, Hastein was led from the city gate to the church where the grave had been prepared. And as the bishop was about to solemnly celebrate mass and all the people listened reverently to the choir songs, the Vikings suddenly leaped beside the coffin and began to shout in their own language that the duke should not be buried.

The Christians, all standing in the church, as if struck by thunder could not understand what was going on. Suddenly Hastein leaped out of the coffin, drew his sword and cut down first the hapless bishop, then the burgrave.

At the same moment the Vikings hurriedly barred the church doors and began the horrendous slaughter of the unarmed Christians. After that they rushed out, killing everyone who stood before them. Finally, those left on the ships also burst into the city and joined in the slaughter.

Running through the streets like invaders and raiding stores and houses, the Vikings grabbed every good that might seem useful to them. Women scouted hiding in cellars were herded into corners and raped, while the surviving children holed up, distraught, in the sewers....

When the blood work was over, God's people were exterminated, taken prisoner or fled. Among the burned houses were piles of corpses, and on every body was evidence of violence; women lay stripped na-

ked, men mutilated. After a few days the stench made all the foulest predators descend from the sky and come out of their dens.

What was left of the living men and women was dragged, laden with chains, to the ships.

The account of the taking of Luni, which we have paraphrased here along the lines suggested by Dudone of St. Quentin, smacks of a macabre fable intended by ecclesiastical chroniclers who always liked to remark on the cruelty of the pagans. But similar expedients for penetrating cities were really used by the Vikings, for example in London and Pleskow (Russia).

Regarding specifically the assault on Luni, Dudon would probably have confused it with London because of an assonance in the name of the two cities: Londonia and Luna.

Probably, the destruction of Luni did not happen as the Historia Normannorum tells. Indeed, it is a work attributable to the fictional genre and considered unreliable by most; but it is known that the description of the dean of St. Quentin rested on a very lively oral tradition, and that besides him, other authors of his contemporaries described it in a similar way.[11]

It is more than likely that it was not the Vikings who sacked and devastated Luni, but the Saracens, who in that period, as we have seen, carried out many piratical actions along the Tyrrhenian coast.

In addition to the Luni legend another unlikely legend about the Vikings is that they allegedly crossed the Mediterranean to Alexandria.

----

[11] Such as Benedict of San Mauro (Gwyn 1977, p. 229).

The ruins of Luni in a nineteenth-century print.

The Bayeux tapestry depicts the building and departure of a Viking fleet.

Vikings in Pisa and along the Arno

Pisa has been famous as a maritime trading centre since Roman times.

It was incorporated into the Marquisate of Tuscany under the Carolingians, and during the reigns of the Berengars and Ottomans it obtained considerable concessions and franchises. As early as the beginning of the 11th century, it appeared as an autonomous municipality. During this period, an impressive fleet was established that sailed the seas with confidence. It is possible that the city's fame and the riches it could hold attracted pirates and invaders who infested the Mediterranean.

As we have seen, the lack of sources prevents us from tracking the Vikings' adventures in Tuscia step by step, partly due to the overlap with legends. However, from the assault on the harbour of Pisa onwards, the events become more credible and realistic, particularly due to the existence of local historical sources and their connection to the stories of well-documented figures.

We will not, I believe, do a disservice to History by adding some narrative description, however consistent with the reality of that era and the data in our possession.

In the summer of 860 rumors of sinister omens reached Pisa.

A decrepit statue of the goddess Juno left in the Forum Square, which the people said represented a Christian saint, had toppled from its pedestal during a windstorm. The wind had blown away even the merchants' stalls: "such phenomena", a passing cleric ruled, "demonstrate our bad deeds toward God's will."

The next morning had brought news that a larger-than-usual pack of wolves had mauled dozens of sheep on the outskirts of town. Fear and superstition aroused even more, making ordinary people tremble.

The air coming from the sea was hot, heavy. The pavement was hot. People walked close to the walls, sheltered from the sun, but by now even the white stones of the houses no longer gave any coolness. In the

The exaltation of Viking warfare in a recent reenacting (photo by Chatigirl, CC 2.0).

useful spaces the boys played. In the verandas of the rich, white-robed maidens and noble ladies laden with jewelry, snoozed lazily or talked slowly among themselves, lying on mats, sipping cherry or raspberry juice from rosy goblets.

In the city no one could yet imagine that the danger of the Norse was already so close: no messenger had arrived in time from France, and it was unthinkable that ships could arrive in such a short time, and right in Pisa.

At that time the mouths of the Arno and the Serchio rivers, flowing together into the Tyrrhenian Sea, promised sailors easy access to the interior. The invaders were as if invited, by the lands themselves, to enter the great lagoon.

Bjørn and Hastein did not take long to settle in. Having taken the jagged estuary they were able to sight, within a short time, the city of Pisa and its market-port. Given the many days at sea and the need for supplies, they decided on a direct, surprise attack, without considering building an encampment.

On that hot summer day the silence was interrupted by a servant shouting about numerous strange barges that were coming up the river, already visible from the highest buildings.

It took the few soldiers of the Marquis of Lucca, Adalbert, who were present in Pisa many minutes to understand what was about to happen and to organize accordingly, while some in the people were already shouting and performing curses, thinking of a Saracen attack.

A few minutes later all hell broke loose. Amid shouting and cackling, wielding axes and swords, the Norse burst into the harbor and pounced on the market, attacking the merchants and the few remaining guards defending the stalls. Anyone who intervened was wiped out with ease, and the soldiers were finished off with axes. Many goods and provisions were already piled up to be loaded later.

The defensive gate of the city had already been closed, but the Vikings were organized for such eventualities. Hastein ordered the small ram off the ship, to prepare it immediately for use. Young Captain Bjørn dictated the tempo for only a few strokes: the Norse force overwhelmed the old sashes in no time.

The Vikings rampaged through the streets, attacking anyone who stood before them and appropriating any valuables. Many men were slaughtered and women, found hiding in cellars or towers, were raped or taken prisoner. The massacre lasted well into the night.

Bishop John III, who took refuge in a chapel in Corte Vecchia, was miraculously saved as the invaders ransacked the ancient baptistery built by the Lombards, appropriating sacred objects.

...Those were not Saracens. Men with blond hair, almost angelic, but with such inhuman ferocity, inflamed by an overwhelming warlike impetus, had never been seen there. Nothing the stunned citizens of Pisa could do against those furies, against this apparent divine punishment.

Collecting a good haul and intoxicated with victory, the furies re-

embarked amid great clamor on their ships adorned with dragon heads, and disappeared, leaving behind a smoldering city.

Ripoli's fort (a hypothesis)

The Vikings pass for skilled builders of defensive walls and fortified villages, as well as improvised but secure forts. After raiding Pisa, they probably built a fortified camp along the Arno River, not too far from the city, to reorganize and establish new strategies.

If the river has not undergone substantial changes in its course, such an encampment could have been located at that great bend in the river, nearby the towns of Ripoli and Musigliano are located today. In fact from this place it is possible to observe the whole bend of the Arno.

Having withdrawn the nimble, shallow-draught snekke from the shore, the Vikings would have raised an earthen embankment by placing pointed wooden logs on top of it. A palisade, extended from one side of the south side to the other, capable of enclosing the bend in the river that would thus have become a kind of river island. In such setting, small ships could have remained even at anchor on the river, being within sight from a simple turret.

From such strategic positions, the Vikings would initiate their rapid raids, striking at villages and towns located along the rivers as well as in the interior of the territories.

Sculptural relief representing the port of Pisa, located on the tower of Pisa. (photo by Sailko, CC 2.5).

Bend of the Arno in the Pisan plain, near the Ponte della Botte between Cascina and Calcinaia (photo taken from Wikiwand.com).

Defensive strategies.
The relics of Saint Zanobi

News of the northern savages' presence soon reached Fiesole (Faesulae) and Florence (Florentia).

Many farmers from the land of San Giovanni, fleeing Gonfolina, arrived at the gates of the Arno city, seeking protection and bearing dire news. They had seen fire, smoke and other ominous signs in the direction of the sea. Some witnesses, who had fled on horseback from Pisa, spoke of avenging angels. The people of Fiesole and Florence feared an imminent invasion, perhaps by the Saracens or of another apocalyptic kind ...

The Marquis of Tuscany Adalbert I, who had moved from Lucca to Florentia, immediately summoned his subordinates and Bishop Andrew. A second call to arms was ordered, involving the young men who lived in the neighborhood of the Posterula Salamoni (near the future Badia Fiorentina), with the aim of garrisoning more of the city walls.

In keeping with centuries-old Christian tradition, the bishop released more fish into the large pool of the church of St. Andrew Prope Arcum.

He also decided to secure what was dearest to the Florentine church and its community: the relics of Bishop Zanobi. The saint had died centuries earlier, in 429, and had been buried in the early church of San Lorenzo...

Bishop Andrew's presence in Florentia is documented in 871 as an imperial envoy, when he sat in judgment together with Marquis Adalbert. In 874 Andrew of Florentia, already strong in important personal relationships even beyond the Alps, obtained from Emperor Ludwig II the Germanic the privilege of immunity for bishop's property.

The bishop is also recorded in 893, when it appears that Andrew's messengers delivered his namesake niece Berta, abbess of the Abbey of St. Andrew, to be educated so that she could one day succeed as abbess herself.

The 9th century was not an easy time. The greatest dangers were called Saracens, Vikings and in the next century Hungarians. The regents of European cities, given the scarcity of military resources, had to face these dangers with strategic actions and reinforcement of fortifications.

In 860, according to Florentine annals, the relics of St. Zanobi, bishop of Florence at the turn of the fourth and fifth centuries, were moved. The sacred remains were taken from the church of San Lorenzo, which was placed at that time outside the defenses of the walls and thus subject to possible attack, to the undoubtedly safer church of Santa Reparata, which was located within the city's wall rectangle.

The procession entered through the Aquilonarum gate, the north-facing one placed in front of the Baptistery, amidst a crowd thronging from all sides, anxious to kiss at least a flap of the blanket that covered the bone remains.

In the confusion the container of relics nicked the branches of a dry elm tree, which miraculously greened up. The custom of planting an elm tree outside churches was very old and of Christian symbolic significance.

Long afterwards, when the tree was cut down, a column was placed there, no doubt from a Roman monument. According to tradition from a piece of the original tree was carved a crucifix now preserved in the church of San Giovannino dei Cavalieri, in Florence on San Gallo Street.

The column of San Zanobi is still visible today in Piazza San Giovanni. It is five meters high, resting on a marble plinth in the center of three stone steps. The capital consists of a simple collar with a cone supporting the marble cross. Attached to the height of the capital is an iron garland with hooks for use of lamps and flowers on holidays.

Domenico Veneziano, Miracle of St. Zanobi, *predella of the S. Lucia de'
Magnoli altarpiece, now in the Fitzwilliam Museum, Cambridge.*

We don't know the year in which the column was erected. We
do know that it was landed by the flood of 1333 and raised the
following year; in 1338 a new cross crowned its top; in 1375 the
inscription recalling the legend of St. Zanobi was added.[12]

On the shaft, in the semicircumference that looks (almost) to
the cathedral, is affixed a wrought-iron elm executed by Migliore
di Niccolò in 1375, commissioned by the pious citizen Tommaso

---

[12] The Latin inscription on the shaft of the column, affixed in 1375 during the time of Bishop
Angelo Ricasoli, shows the date of the year 409 (ANNO AB INCARNATIONE DOMINI
CCCC.VIIII.), relating to the miracle of the elm: QUAM CUM FERETRUM SANCTI COR-
PORIS TETIGISSET SUBITO FRONDES ET FLORES MIRACULOSA PRODUXIT.
The information is not accurate, however, as Zanobi at that time was still alive and would have
been alive for another twenty years. Moreover, the sacred relics could have had no other worthy
home than San Lorenzo because at that date there was no Christian church within the walls of
Florentia. The cathedral of Santa Reparata would be built in the 6th century, in the time of Theo-
doric, and was perhaps, initially, of the Arian confession.

di Bernardo Viviani.

The cross fell to the ground again in 1501, during preparations for the feast of S. Giovanni.

The episode of the elm tree is narrated in octave rhyme by the proponent of the "volgar fiorentino" Pierfrancesco Giambullari (1495-1555), canon of San Lorenzo:

At the Piazza del Duomo at the entrance
There was a great dry elm standing upright
So that passing, by a wave given
The gurney somewhat to the elm yields:
Nor first touched it had it that shown
Miraculous thing was as is seen,
That the dry elm in an instant out
All covered was with fronds and flowers.

The poet continues to narrate and concludes thus:

Placed there was that column in sign
And in memory of the worthy miracle.

On January 26 each year, commemorating the translation of the "Most Glorious Bishop and Protector of the City," a garland of white and red carnations the heraldic colors of Florence is placed at the base of the column.

But why, during a terrible raid like the Viking raid, would a medieval bishop have bothered to save the ancient relics of a saint who lived more than four centuries earlier?

In the early 5th century Zanobi had done his best to defend the city against the hordes of the barbarian Radagasius, by inciting the people to fearlessly resist with prayer and deeds, so much so that the victory and capture of the barbarian was considered the work of divine providence.

Probably Bishop Andrew, in the 9th century, trusted in further

San Zanobi's column today, surrounded by tourists, in Florence's Piazza San Giovanni.

intercession of the holy bishop Zanobi. That is why his relics were brought just then, at the time of the Viking invasion, inside the city. Thus, when we look at the column in S. Giovanni Square, we can also think of the Norse invaders and the terror they brought to our region.

But ingratiating themselves into the favor of St. Zanobi was, of course, not the only strategic action of the bishop and Marquis Adalbert.

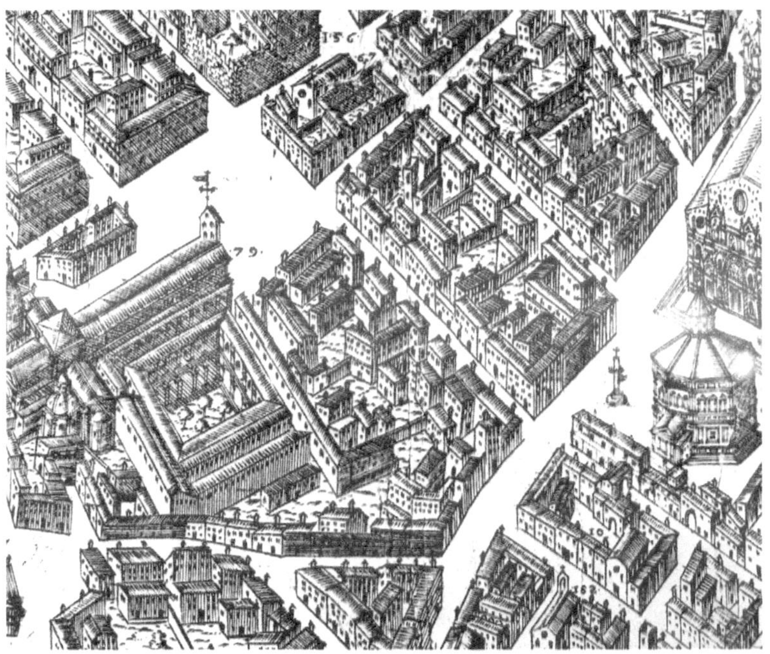

Detail of Stefano Buonsignori's plan, 1584/1594 showing the church of San Lorenzo, the column of San Zanobi and the Baptistery.

The statue of Saint Zanobi visible in the frame of the facade of Santa Maria del Fiore.

The "Chain". The clashes on the Arno

During the swift sacking of Pisa, the Vikings captured some Christian clerics. From them, they learned that if they sailed upstream for two days, they would find a valley with many farms, as well as two cities: one on the river and one on the hill above.

Hastein, Bjørn and the other chieftains had already decided to sail up the Arno and continue burning farms; the existence of these twin cities could provide a definite goal. After sacking Faesulae and Florentia, they could consider taking further action, perhaps reaching Rome itself in the hope of being joined by other Norse warriors for a more effective siege.

With the usual speed and determination, ships and everything needed for sustenance and, above all, for sieges were organized. Hastein decided to leave part of his men in the encampment on the bend of the Arno, not far from Pisa, which would be the base for returning to the sea, following a pattern already applied on the Rhone. Bjørn and his men, young and thirsty for enterprise, would initiate actions against the two cities. But much could not yet be decided, for the territories were totally unknown to the invaders.

On their way up the river the Vikings passed through a territory composed of richly wooded agri-lands alternating with olive groves, vineyards and wheat fields cultivated by the Italics and the servants of the Lombard nobles; but they also often noticed vast uncultivated lands, a paradise for wild boars and wolves, abandoned and now decaying farms. They did not need patrols to protect the ships coming up the river.

They therefore reached the height of the hill of San Miniato (now in the province of Pisa), where at that time there was a church founded by the Lombards in the previous century. The Viking lookouts noticed the presence, at the water's edge, of a large swinging

River chains began to be used right around the time of the ninth-century invasions and never fell into disuse. Here we see an example in a 17th-century English print.

chain that would have obstructed the passage to any kind of boat.

This was one of the few forms of protection against invaders from the sea that had proved useful in other contexts (especially in Northern Europe, against the Vikings themselves). Marquis Adalbert had given the order to activate this barrier, and some soldiers quickly went to the site to act. These barely made it to the location, which is still called La Catena[13] today, and then fled to the nearby hills. To their surprise, they had already sighted, the vanguards of the Viking fleet.

The Vikings, accosting one of the snekke on the right bank, dismounted some warriors who guardedly went to ascertain the difficulty. Noting the absence of any garrison, they immediately undertook to

---

[13] This stretch of the Arno would have lent itself to preventing the continuation of Viking ships. The first medieval mention of the locality bore the name Bacula or Obacula from the Bacoli stream that flows down into the Arno. The place-name Catena was later established for having been for centuries a border place between Pisa and Florence where a "chain" was located to control goods. But it is possible that some kind of barrier existed in earlier centuries.

remove the obstacle. They broke with sturdy clubs the cogwheel of the winch that supported the chain, causing it to sink completely into the riverbed.

This was how the Vikings were able to continue their ascent while the Tuscan sentries galloped off to inform their commanders. The expedient of the chain, which was supposed to allow a little more time for organizing resistance, had proved completely ineffective....

Having passed an area where the river flowed close to some hills,[14] the invaders finally found the first armed resistance from the Tuscan army.

A group of soldiers from the city of Florentia had lurked on one of the two banks with some small catapults. Several pignatte, large containers with naphtha, pitch and sulfur, were thrown at the ships, and soon after incendiary arrows were fired. Going up the Arno against the current, but with a strong libeccio wind and with the sail set, the speed of the ships was so great that the launchers missed the majority of the launches. Only one ship was hit.

Enraged by the attack, when they reached the confluence of a right tributary of the Arno,[15] the Vikings made a short ascent as far as they could and set about killing poor shepherds, setting fire to their huts, capturing their women and several head of cattle. Some of the peasants were sacrificed at a tree.

Having chosen a large oak tree, the Northerners drew a sacred fence and performed the cultic ceremony according to fixed rules consecrated by their tradition. They took those despairing people and, brought beside the trunk of the tree, stabbed them with a spear. Others were hanged and left hanging on the tree.

After that, mead flowed down in torrents.

---

[14] This would be the so-called Gonfolina. This term is used to indicate an inlet of a river and in our case the narrows of the Arno River that corresponds to the delimitation between Upper and Lower Valdarno, in the municipality of Lastra a Signa, not far from the confluence of the Ombrone stream.

[15] We are talking about the Ombrone River.

The copious libations belonged to a magical region. The goiter embraced, in the sacrificial feast, heaven and earth. The more the alcohol clouded minds the more the warriors felt close to the gods of Vallalla. Drunk, they chanted chewing the acorns of the oak tree to ward off the evils that prevented the sperm from sprouting in women's wombs.

After the night's hangover they resumed navigation, lapped another waterway on their left but preferred to stay in the bed of the great river.

By now they had reached the end of the navigable route and the two large cities, with rich opportunities for plunder...were ready to receive them.

The riverbed blurred between marshes and swampy terrain. Fresh air vibrated in the great green basin mottled with scattered white huts, in the blue of the mountains around, little less intense than the blue of the sky.

Young Bjørn on the bow of the first snekke, beside the griffin figurehead, carefully scanned the horizon. In his soul, pride, ambition, love of novelty and desire for violence had tumulted together.

Finally, Florentia appeared at the end of the valley.

Its sun-beamed red brick walls conveyed their sturdiness, the round towers that flanked the large gates looked like giants ready to interdict passage.

Later, on the hills to the upper left, the city of Fiesole came into view.

The Vikings anchored their snekke long before the city's vanguards on the Arno and nimbly landed on the right bank of the river.

Bjørn and Hastein immediately ordered a fortified camp to be built over an extensive rise of sandy ground, surrounded by marshes, just before the confluence of a stream. At the same time, numerous scouts were immediately sent to study the area around the cities more closely.

Others went hunting in the lush woods at the foot of the hills. In the evening some large wild boars were roasted. The smell of the libations reached as far as the west gate of Florentia, arousing the suspicions of the inhabitants while the garrisons had already been warned of the threat that had been going on for several hours.

During the evening the actions to be taken to conquer the two cities were decided. Faesulae and the large castle at its foot were considered more affordable. The city's ancient walls were still shattered in several places from the time of the Gothic wars and were badly restored. The city of Florentia would taste the Viking axe soon after.

On the steep slope of the Fiesole mountain that precipitates toward the narrow valley of the Mugnone stood a large manor house, the residence of Bishop Donatus of Fiesole.

It was shortly after dawn and the religious, together with Bishop Donatus were preparing for the recitation of daily services, after which they would remain in the castle, without spreading the faith in the countryside, their usual mission. For it had been known for some days that the city of Pisa had been stormed, sacked, and set on fire by a horde of giant, bloodthirsty warriors, and that these were now coming up the river.

A Florentine emissary had arrived and confirmed that the mysterious invaders had taken camp in the valley below.

Bishop Donato, the sack of Fiesole and of the bishop's castle Fiesole

Bishop Donatus was a mysterious and intriguing character who was close to Pope Leo IV and Emperors Lothair I and Ludovic II. Shortly after the events recounted in this book, he left for the Roman Council of 861, which was convened by Pope Nicholas I to judge Archbishop John VII of Ravenna, who had been accused of abusing his power by his suffragan bishops.

In 816, Donatus, the son of Irish Christians, abandoned his family in search of greater religious fervour and wandered through Europe, reaching as far as Rome. Upon returning to his homeland, he stopped in Fiesole at a time when the clergy and people, following the death of Bishop Grasulfo, had to elect a new bishop. Impressed by Donatus' eloquence and guided by divine inspiration, the Fiesolans chose the unknown pilgrim, who was initially reluctant but ultimately yielded to their wishes.

The Irish clergyman, also sometimes remembered as a Scot, became bishop of Fiesole in 829 and governed the diocese for a very long period, until 876. He gave himself with supreme zeal to the government of the Fiesole church, took particular care of the instruction of its clergy, gathering around him a good number of disciples whom he educated not only in the theological disciplines and grammar, but, considering the age in which they lived, full of dangers and overpowering, also in the military art of war.

Accompanied on the journey to Rome by his disciple Andrea Scoto[16] he brought a wind of culture and enthusiasm to the Fiesole diocese on his return. The new bishop did not content himself with recovering the goods of which the Fiesole church had been robbed by vassals and some religious predecessors but, knowing Virgil, made the mythology of the ancients dear again to the

---

[16] Irish religious were often given the name Scotus. Andrew was appointed archdeacon of Fiesole by Donatus himself. He joined him as a close collaborator and became his trusted man for the most delicate matters of diocesan administration.

ninth-century generations. In the verses he wrote (which preceded the biography of St. Bridget, his compatriot and also a fellow traveler to Rome) Democritus and Hesiod are mentioned. Even after several centuries his poetic works were held in high esteem.

The industriousness as "teacher" of the northern bishop must have been effective in many future manifestations of Fiesole intellectual life. From a 1018 memoir preserved for us by the Annals of the Camaldolese Order, we learn that even at that time there continued to be in Fiesole the priest assigned to the teaching of grammar, that is, letters: «*Etiam in Ecclesia Fesulana Grammatici titulus, quo ornabatur Theuzus fesulanae Ecclesiae primicerius in privilegio Regembaldi Fesularum Episcopi ab anno 1018 spectante*».[17]

Under Donatus, in 854, the county of Fiesole had been merged with that of Florence, but although Donatus lost political and fiscal jurisdiction over the territory of the former county, he managed to retain sovereignty over the city under the bishop's jurisdiction. He also obtained the county of Turicchi in Val di Sieve; thus Donato was the last of the counts of Fiesole and the first of the counts of Turicchi.

The albeit fragmentary news coming to us from the darkness of the early Middle Ages confirms Donato in an intense and constant alliance with the rulers of Italy. And all the more true is the praise of faithful servant that is bestowed, in his tombstone, on this bishop-warrior who at times even sided against the Pope:

> HIC EGO DONATUS SCOTORUM SANGUINE CRETUS SOLUS, IN HOC MOUND, POWDER WORM VOROR.
> REGIBUS ITALICIS SERVIVI PLURIBUS ANNIS. LOTHARIO THE GREAT, LODOVICOQUE BONO OCTONES LUSTRIS SEPTENIS INSUPER ANNIS POST, FESULANA PRAESUL, IN URBE FUI. FREE DISCIPULIS DICTABAM SCRIPTA LIBELLIS, SCHEMATE METRORUM, DICTA BEATA SENUM.

---

[17] G. B. Mittarelli, A. Costadoni, *Annales Camaldulenses (...)*, Venezia 1760, I, p. 301.

PARCE VIATOR, ADIS QUISQUIS PRO MUNERE
CHRISTO, TE MODO NON PIGEAT CERNERE BUSTA
MEA, ATQUE PRECARE DEUM, RESIDET QUI CULMI-
NE COELI, UT MIHI CONCEDAT REGNA BEATA SUA.

(Acta Sanctorum, 22 Oct. IX. 662)

Many elements suggest that Bishop Donatus had a warlike temperament and a daring spirit, on a par with other clergy figures of the time, just as they have been redrawn in recent movie reconstructions.

In 844, Sergius II, from a noble Roman family, had been appointed pontiff sine nomina imperatoris. With the aim of asserting sovereign authority in the very seat of Christianity, Emperor Lothair sent his son Ludovic at the head of a large army. As the army passed through Florentine territory, the bishop of Fiesole joined the expedition at the head of his own armigers.

Again in 850, when Ludwig himself was crowned emperor by Pope Leo IV, we find Donatus of Fiesole, together with the bishop of Florence (Gerard), traveling to Rome to sit in judgment with the pope and the emperor in deciding a dispute between the bishops of Arezzo and Siena.

Pope Leo, later sanctified, was the one who worked to defend Rome from the threats of Saracen incursions by having a fortified wall built around the Vatican and creating the so-called "Leonine city."

Perhaps Bishop Donatus' presence in Rome was not simply clerical but also strategic and warlike. Evidently Donatus of Fiesole was also a warrior and in addition to the cross he firmly wielded the sword. Whichever way it went, the Church sanctified him.

Bishop Donatus having enriched and honored the Church and Bishopric of Fiesole, he went to receive the merits of his office in Heaven on the twenty-second day of October (876), on which is by the Roman Martyrology placed his feast day.[18]

---

[18] In the early 19th century, Bishop Ranieri Mancini ordered Donato's sacred remains to be

*St. Donatus of Fiesole in a painting by Andrea del Verroc-
chio, visible in the Fiesole cathedral.*

But let us return to the time of the arrival of the Vikings in the
Florentine valley.

*After the mass celebrated in the castle chapel two servants helped the
bishop with preparations for the defense of the city.*

*Donatus slipped on his linen shirt and cloth breeches, while a ser-
vant fastened the leggings around his calves. Then he donned the felt
jacke, the leather bodice, the chain mail surplice with the red cloth tunic
over it embroidered with his insignia, with the image of an "andante
lion". He hung his Lombard sword from his shoulder belt and went out
to the tower to watch the enemy advance.*

transferred from the Badia Fiesolana to the cathedral of San Romolo (erected on the hill in 1028
by Bishop Jacopo il Bavaro) in a chapel dedicated to him to the left of the high altar, next to the
monumental chapel of Bishop Leonardo Salutati.

The soldiers available to the bishop were few, consequently it was decided to remain barricaded inside the castle.

Throughout that late August day the Viking tried to penetrate Fiesole. About a hundred warriors were forcing the south gate, the one looking toward the valley of Florentia; others were trying to set fire to some sections of the wooden walls. The inhabitants and soldiers present managed to cope momentarily with each attempted raid.

At a later stage the Vikings, making a thorough check of the walls, found a more approachable and poorly defended section on the eastern hill, near the church of St. Apollinare.

The use of a battering ram and a few harpoons sufficed at that point, since the walls were poorly defended. Too vast and tortuous was the walled perimeter of the ancient city for such a small number of armigers.

The sentries gave immediate alarm, but it quickly became clear that the only option left was to hide or flee.

Thus it was that the Northerners penetrated inside the city. Also in Fiesole, as in Pisa, they looted, killed, and burned, almost as if it were a divine punishment.

Some citizens managed to escape through the north gate and hide in the surrounding hills, such as in the caves of Montereggi, above the limaria pool of the now-abandoned Roman aqueduct; many were instead captured, locked up in the theater and killed with arrows and spears.

Still others were burned alive amid heartrending screams in the burning of the Paleo-Christian church that had replaced the Etruscan College of Augurs, once overlooking the Roman Forum.

After the sacking of Fiesole, the Vikings focused their attention on the other objective: the residence of the bishop, the castle that faced south, at the foot of the city of Faesulae, near today's Badia Fiesolana.

The Bishop's castle was well defended and strategically placed.
For two full days the siege took place without any notable events,

except sporadic attempts. The Vikings already seemed satisfied with the loot stolen from the city and not too excited about suffering further losses.

It looked like it would take some time. The attackers set up camp a few dozen yards from the walls to assess the circumstances. The bishop-count's clerics and soldiers began to hope for some breathing space, perhaps to be able to start negotiations and drive the Vikings away with a simple fee.

But on the third night the count, when he had just managed to get to sleep, was jolted awake by a commotion of confusion.

"The Vikings, the Vikings!"

"They are already inside the castle, they have taken the guards of the southern wall from behind. They climbed up the cliff. They found a way!"

All the clergymen and soldiers barricaded themselves in the castle keep. It was necessary to shield the bishop.

Donatus wielded his sword. His men tried to block access to the rooms. But the rush of the throng succeeded in breaking through the main door.

A gleam among the lit flashlights, a cry from a soldier, then thuds and shouts. The garrison leader, sword drawn and face bloodied, stood before the bishop fighting three Vikings.

Donatus, an expert in weapons, also milled his sword and got busy: a giant Viking came at him, but the bishop instead of retreating in the face of the whirlwind of lunges and slashes advanced and avoided the sword and struck the assailant in the belly.

But other swords and axes threatened. While the Vikings were distracted by his men, the bishop managed to get away through a passageway that led from the chapel of Saints Peter and Romulus to the castle stables, he walked along a dark corridor where one barely passed one at a time, straddled a horse and galloped toward nearby Florentia.

Meanwhile in the castle the fight was short and fierce. Those who were wounded were finished off with bearded axes.[19] *Eager for booty,*

---

[19] Already in Eastern civilizations and the Mediterranean world, the axe had a special cha-

the invaders seized the church treasury, destroyed the bishopric library, looted cellars and storerooms, slaughtered oxen and sheep in pens, and set the whole building on fire.

Bishop Donatus, spurring his steed into a wild ride managed to ride smoothly the few miles that separated him from Florentia. Received by Duke Adalbert he communicated what had happened to the castle seat of the Fiesole diocese.

Florentia locked and reinforced the large gates. Only the solid walls could protect the citizens and fugitives from the surrounding area from the rapacious Vikings to whom the unguarded territory had been left at their mercy.

---

racter as a political and religious symbol, as it did in Crete in the Minoan age and in Nuragic Sardinia. The axe, as well as a tool for work and war, was undoubtedly the weapon of those in command, as can be deduced from the relief depictions on the Etruscan stelae of Larth Ninie of Fiesole and Avele Feluske of Volterra.

The area facing the Badia Fiesolana, where Bishop Donato's castle stood, in an early 18th-century painting.

Badia Fiesolana as seen from the "Bolognese" road.

The siege of Florence

According to tradition, during the reign of Charlemagne, Florence experienced rapid economic and building development after finding peace and relative justice. The legend of the city's destruction by Attila and the subsequent reconstruction ordered by the emperor himself indicates how city life, which had almost been extinguished under the Goths and Byzantines, flourished again with the arrival of the Franks.

During the great Viking raids, Florence was a major settlement in the peninsula, with solid walls that had reoccupied the entire Roman square after shrinking in the 6th century, extending further towards the Arno. Its population must have been around ten thousand.

The evening following the capture of the bishop's castle in Fiesole, as an unbearable sultriness stagnated over the city, wagons overflowing with the wounded arrived; the iron grating of the North Gate was stopped at half height, and the massive wooden gate was reopened to let the last desperate people inside.

The Florentine Bishop Andrew and the Count-Bishop of Faesulae sadly followed from the galleries of the walls the destruction and fires around the city. The rage on nearby Monticulus St. Laurentis was particularly violent: the church fire gave off a column of smoke higher than the others, almost rivaling that still smouldering at the foot of Faesulae's hill. The Viking burned fields, houses, huts, stables.

Occasionally a few groups of Norsemen would approach the walls, but out of reach of the arches, making obscene gestures and taunting the sentries in that unintelligible language.

The Florentines, given the few hundred soldiers at their disposal, could not afford an outflow to confront those superior beings on a warlike level. The only possible defense consisted in keeping the city gates firmly closed and waiting for the Vikings to be satiated in the material misappropriation of objects, food and livestock, which, by now out of

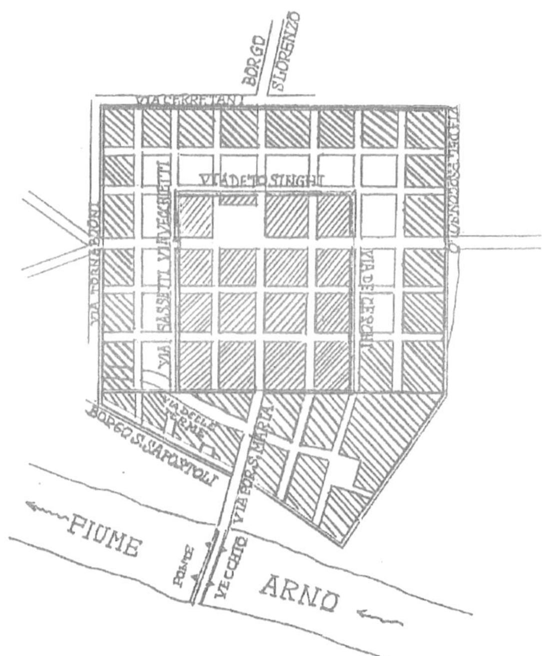

The "Carolingian" city wall . Author's drawing (1989).

control, were scampering haphazardly across the plain.

Two messengers were sent to Arezzo to ask for help from Bishop Pietro, who was also an upright warrior.

The days went by uncertainly. Bjørn continued to reason about how to get past the city walls, every section of which he had now analyzed. But there was a new problem to contend with: the warriors, besides being satiated with booty and libations, were beginning to be tired. Long had been the epic of this expedition, from the moment it had been decided to reach the Mediterranean; many had been the raids, the conquests but also the human losses. Certainly, for many among the Norse this could have been enough, and perhaps Hastein was among them. Loaded onto ships with the fruits of the raids, the invaders could have returned to the fort located toward the mouth of the Arno, to make arrangements for reaching a new destination, perhaps Rome itself...or for a possible return north.

The ancient structure of the Pagliazza tower, a vestige of the "Byzantine" city wall. Photo by the author (1988).

Yet there was still an inspiration, a typically Viking temperament, that drove most to seek confrontation, conquest, glory.

One afternoon a Viking masnada led by Bjørn Ironsides concentrated under the walls of Florentia, attempting to penetrate the city from the southern gate, the one adjacent to the Arno River.

Duke Adalbert had been informed that the southern gate was the most fragile and at that time least defended. It was inevitable to attempt a sortie, hoping to surprise the Vikings. A group of picked soldiers came out of the west gate to take the enemy from behind. They were to be joined by the horsemen of Bishop Peter of Arezzo who had reached the hills upstream from Florence in the night and responded to the light signals of the sentries.

Shortly thereafter outside the walls the battle was ignited; on both sides furious warriors clashed amidst a great din of arms, each man fighting on his own, without a predetermined plan, relying on the chance of the moment, the strength of his arm, skill in the sword or in handling the axe. Behind the invaders came shortly the Aretine horsemen who were intercepted near the bridge over the Arno.

The impact between these forces was most violent, and in the following scuffles many wounded on both sides fell into the river, drowning. The encircling action made it possible to break the intensity of the Viking attack, but in the meantime, though reduced in numbers, the Norse got the better of the Florentines, forcing them to retreat and flee.

Soon after, energized by the clash, they took to striking the south gate with a large, long log coiffed like a battering ram, which Bjørn had made especially for the gates of Florentia.

From the two towers that flanked the gate everything was thrown. First, boiling water and oil. Then a group of young men, armed for the purpose, intervened with a dense stone pelting as the soldiers poured their full ammunition of arrows toward the attackers. The intensity of this action dealt a blow to the progress of the attack, causing the group of Norse to leave.

One morning near the end of August, the elements suddenly broke out and a very thick rain began to fall.

As the hailstones tapped the stones of the city of Florentia, the Vikings, now satiated with the stolen riches and considering the difficulty of being able to penetrate the city, decided to fall back toward the mouth of the Arno.

Bjørn's men, those who still had the most eagerness for conquest, were persuaded with a promise to consider new actions and raids further south, toward Roman territory. But Hastein was already clear that there was unlikely to be a Viking "sack" in Rome.

The invaders, thus vanished. According to some, it was perhaps at this time that they decided to head for the ancient and wealthy city of Luni, but as we have seen, that action mostly corresponds to a legend.

Florentia was thus spared, only its territory tasted Viking bestial ferocity.

Bishop Donatus and everyone else could breathe a bitter sigh of relief. That summer of blood and death that had terrorized Florentia and Tuscany, devastated the city of Faesulae and the entire 'bishopric building, slaughtered all the religious of the Fiesole diocese in an instant, was over!

But in indelible memory of the devastation, the year following the Viking raids many rubicund and beautiful blond children were born in the villages along the Arno River.

Historical conclusions

Since the Middle Ages, the name 'Viking' has been used to describe rough, violent men from the north who were tall, blond and rugged. They wore animal skins and were ready to turn to violence at the slightest provocation. But there is more to it than that. Delving into Norse history reveals what the world owes to the Vikings: the discovery of new routes and the establishment of trade centres; the settlement of remote places such as the Faroe Islands, Shetland, Iceland and Greenland; and the creation of efficient and powerful states such as Kievan Rus' and the Duchy of Normandy.

It was precisely from Normandy that William the Conqueror left for England, while another Norman, Robert Guiscard, obtained the recognition of 'vassal of the Holy Cross' and the title of 'Duke of Apulia, Calabria and future Duke of Sicily' from the Pope (Nicholas II of Florence) in the 11th century.

Moreover, although in the previous pages we have described the ferocity and indifference to the death of strangers, it is not difficult to show, at the same time, how much a Viking's existence was marked by contemplation, spirituality and feelings. It is perhaps in this paradox that much of the success that the Vikings achieve today - in an age so full of contradictions - is played out through film and literature.

The Havamal, the sacred text of the ancient Vikings, gives us a glimpse of their conception of existence: advice on how to live, on friendship, on how to treat guests; on prudence and moderation in dealing with different situations, in politics and in war.

The winters were long and cold, and the Viking family spent several months and endless evenings locked in their homes. While the dreadful north wind blew outside, the northern lights performed their flickers, and the wavering firelight made manual labor difficult (such as weaving for women, or repairing work or war tools for men), the Vikings had nothing but themselves and their fellow humans to reflect on and reflect themselves.

The home was thus, more than in other human worlds, an ideal social place to celebrate banquets and sacraments, to participate in the long vigils at which plans were made for spring expeditions, occasions when "scaldi" (poets) and orators became the protagonists. In the long winter night people were entertained in different ways, some board games were played, for example "checkers" or "fox and goose" but even more so chess (originating in India, they were introduced to Europe by the Arabs becoming very popular in the North).

From an early age children were taught that the family of which they were members also constituted a small military unit, in which powers were concentrated on the leader who could decide, in the face of mistakes made, even on their own lives. The women themselves were ready to take up arms at any eventuality, and the adoles were already warriors in their own right.

Marriages were arranged between the heads of the family clans but conflicts could arise if the desires of the young differed from those of the parents. It was therefore once again to one's own family that one was accountable and in whom one sought understanding. Each individual remained connected to the family in any situation, receiving support in difficult times in life, but with a moral obligation to always help his lineage.

The Vikings favored satire but became very touchy when it was directed against themselves: The Havamal are full of ironic wit about hospitality, for example. We read, "He welcomes me as a guest only if I need to eat nothing or if two legs of mutton still hang from the ceiling when I have eaten only one." We can say, given the nicknames that have come down to us, that the Vikings had a predilection to pick up on the quirks or flaws of their fellow man: see for example Ragnar Lodbrok ("Hairy Arms"), Aroldo Blue Tooth, Svend Forked Beard, and other nicknames such as "cat's back" or "dog's mouth." Many of these nicknames were related to physical deformities: Ivar Boneless or Sigurd Snake-in-the-Eye, for example. Sometimes the epithet was paradoxical:

'Tord the Short' was exceptionally tall, and a dark-skinned man might be called 'the Blond' in contrast.

In this ironic respect, perhaps the Vikings might be seen as similar to the Tuscans ...

Bibliography

Ancient sources

Abbone di S. Germano, *De bellis Parisiacae urbis*
Adamo da Brema, *Gesta Hammaburgensis Ecclesiae Pontificum*
Alfredo il Grande, *Cronaca Anglosassone*
Amato di Montecassino, *Historia Normannorum*
Costantino Porfirogenito, *Geoponica*
Al Bakri, *"Geografia". Libro delle strade e dei domini*
Dudone di San Quintino, *Historia Normannorum*
Ermentario, *Translatio S. Filiberti*
Ibn Fadlan, *Manoscritto*, Diario delle ambascerie
Magnus Olaus, *Historia delle genti et della natura delle cose settentrionali*
Prudenzio di Troyes, *Annales Bertiniani (suite)*
Snorri Sturluson, *Edda* (a cura di Gianna Chiesa Isnardi, TEA, Milano 1997)
Vita Donati, *Acta Sanctorum* 22 Ottobre. IX. 662

Bibliography

AA. VV., *Enciclopedia cattolica*, Città del Vaticano, Sansoni, Firenze 1948-1954
AA. VV. , *L'Italia Storica*, Touring Club Italiano, Conosci l'Italia, Milano 1961
Ibid., Guide l'Italia, *Firenze e dintorni*, Milano 1974
Ibid., Gude l'Italia, *Toscana*, Milano 2005
Ammirato Scipione, *Vescovi di Fiesole, di Volterra e d'Arezzo*, Firenze 1637
Bargellini Piero, *La splendida storia di Firenze*, Vallecchi, Firenze 1964

Barbadoro Bernardino, *La via dei secoli*, vol. II, Le Monnier, Firenze 1953

Bloch Raymond, *Gli Etruschi*, Il Saggiatore, Milano 1959

Brøndsted Johannes, *I Vichinghi*, Einaudi, Torino 2001

Brunori Dionisio, *Il Seminario di Fiesole*, Tipografia Rigacci, Fiesole 1925

Carocci Guido, *I dintorni di Firenze*, Società Multigrafica Editrice, Roma 1968 (prima edizione: Firenze, 1907)

Cohat Yves, I *Vichinghi signori del mare*, Electa, Torino 1993

Davidsohn Robert, *Storia di Firenze*, vol. I, Sansoni 1956

De Agostino Alberto, *Populonia. La città e la necropoli.* Istituto poligrafico dello Stato, 1965.

Delogu Paolo, *I Normanni in Italia*, Liguori Editore, Napoli 1990

Di Mauro Nicola, *Normanni, i predoni venuti da nord*, Giunti, Firenze 2003

Gwyn Jones, *I Vichinghi, avventura di una civiltà*, Newton Compton editori, Roma 1977

Holger Arbman, *I Vichinghi,* il Saggiatore, Milano 1969

Lindsay Jack, *I Normanni*, Rizzoli, Milano 1984

Lopes Pegna Mario, *Firenze dalle origini al medioevo*, Del Re Editore, Firenze 1974

Marini Giuseppe, *Letteratura Latina*, Mursia, Milano 1995

Matthew Donald, *L'Europa Normanna*, Jouvence, Roma 1987

Pallottino Massimo, *Etruscologia*, Milano 1968 (VI ed.)

Pecchioni Enio, *La Storia di Fiesole*, SP44, Firenze 1979

Pescetti Angelo, *Compendio della vita di S. Andrea di Scozia*, Firenze 1805

Pörtner Rudolph, *L'epopea dei Vichinghi*, Garzanti, Milano 1972

Puccinelli Placido, *Vita e azioni del Beato Andrea di Scozia*, Onofri, Firenze 1676

Saitta Armando, *Il cammino umano*, vol. I, La Nuova Italia, Firenze 1962

Thompson Edward Arthur, *Attila e gli Unni*, Sansoni, Firenze 1963

Tommasini Anselmo Maria, *I Santi Irlandesi in Italia*, Vita e Pensiero, Milano 1932

Shippey Tom, - *Vita e morte dei Grandi Vichinghi*, Odoya, Bologna 2018

Stewart Gordon, *When Asia was the World: Traveling Merchants, Scholars, Warriors, and Monks who created the "Riches of the East"*, Da Capo Press - Perseus Books, 2009.

Contents

Florence, 2020

www.ingramcontent.com/pod-product-compliance
Lightning Source LLC
Chambersburg PA
CBHW020132180726
47992CB00022B/2613